RUSSELL PUBLIC LIBRARY

S0-ADP-570

C-
975.2
Jy

Joseph

Maryland

DATE DUE

1998	

DISCARDED

PRINTED IN U.S.A.

RUSSELL PUBLIC LIBRARY
32715

C-
975.2
Jy

The United States

Maryland

Paul Joseph
ABDO & Daughters

visit us at
www.abdopub.com

Published by Abdo & Daughters, 4940 Viking Drive, Suite 622, Edina, Minnesota 55435.
Copyright © 1998 by Abdo Consulting Group, Inc., Pentagon Tower, P.O. Box 36036,
Minneapolis, Minnesota 55435 USA. International copyrights reserved in all countries.
No part of this book may be reproduced in any form without written permission from the
publisher.

Printed in the United States.

Cover and Interior Photo credits: Super Stock, Peter Arnold, Inc., Corbis-Bettmann, Wide
World

Edited by Lori Kinstad Pupeza
Contributing editor Brooke Henderson
Special thanks to our Checkerboard Kids—Gracie Hansen, Peter Rengstorf, Peter Dumdei,
Stephanie McKenna

All statistics taken from the 1990 census; The Rand McNally Discovery Atlas of The
United States. Other sources: Compton's Encyclopedia, 1997; *Maryland*, Heinrichs,
Children's Press, Chicago, 1989.

Library of Congress Cataloging-in-Publication Data

Joseph, Paul, 1970-
    Maryland / Paul Joseph.
    p. cm. -- (United States)
    Includes index.
    ISBN 1-56239-881-4
    1. Maryland--Juvenile literature. [1. Maryland.] I. Title. II. Series: United
States (Series).
    F181.3.J67 1998
    975.2--dc21
                                        97-23901
                                        CIP
                                        AC

Contents

Welcome to Maryland

The state of Maryland can be found in the eastern United States on the **Atlantic Ocean**. Besides the Atlantic Ocean, Maryland is **bordered** by the states of Delaware, Pennsylvania, West Virginia, and Virginia. On the west side of Maryland is the nation's capital, Washington D.C.

The beautiful state of Maryland has thick forests, rugged mountains, excellent farmland, and scenic shores. It is also a very historic state with many monuments to famous people and events.

Maryland was one of the 13 original states in the Union. The state was named for Queen Henrietta Maria, the wife of Charles I of England in 1632.

The state's nickname is the "Old Line State." The name was given by George Washington who admired the state's fighting in the **American Revolution**. It is said that nothing got by the line of Maryland.

Today, Maryland attracts many visitors to its state. The beautiful land, monuments, cities, and people make it a popular place for **tourists** to visit.

Weekend sailing races in Chesapeake Bay.

Fast Facts

MARYLAND

Capital
Annapolis (33,187 people)
Area
9,838 square miles
(25,480 sq km)
Population
4,798,622 people
Rank: 19th
Statehood
April 28, 1788
(7th state admitted)
Principal rivers
Patuxent River, Potomac River
Highest point
Backbone Mountain;
3,360 feet (1,024 m.)
Largest city
Baltimore (736,014 people)
Motto
Fatti maschii, parole femine
(Manly deeds, womanly words)
Song
"Maryland, My Maryland"
Famous People
Benjamin Banneker, Frederick
Douglas, Francis Scott Key,
George Herman "Babe" Ruth,
Upton Sinclair

Maryland is one of the original 13 colonies

13

*S*tate Flag

*B*altimore Oriole

*B*lack-eyed Susan

*W*hite Oak

About Maryland
The Old Line State

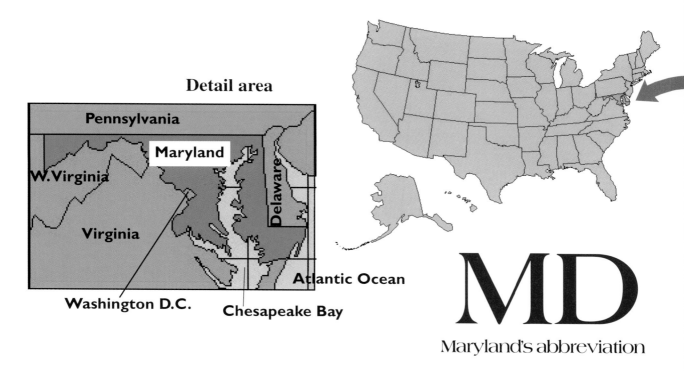

Detail area

Pennsylvania

Maryland

W. Virginia

Virginia

Delaware

Atlantic Ocean

Washington D.C.

Chesapeake Bay

MD
Maryland's abbreviation

Borders: west (Virginia, West Virginia, Washington D.C.), north (Pennsylvania), east (Delaware, Atlantic Ocean), south (Virginia, Chesapeake Bay)

Nature's Treasures

Even though Maryland is small, it has many wonderful treasures in its state. There are breathtaking mountains, scenic lakes and rivers, beautiful national parks, thick forests, and the wonderful coast of the **Atlantic Ocean**.

The state has rich, **fertile** soil in many areas and **minerals** under the ground. Many different fish swim in the rivers and on the coast of the Atlantic Ocean. More than 45 percent of Maryland's land has forests on it. Some of the trees that grow there are pine and oak.

Maryland has a wide range of climates that attract many visitors to the state. In the summers, people can find cool temperatures in the mountain areas. Along the coast people can find very warm weather, making it a great vacation area. In the winter months, snow falls throughout the state.

Not too many states offer as many different treasures as Maryland. Because of the land, water, and other treasures in the state, people from around the world visit this wonderful area.

People come to Maryland to enjoy the beauty of its shoreline.

Beginnings

The first known people to live in Maryland were **Native Americans**. They were the Susquehanna, the Piscataway, and the Nanticoke. By the 1700s, all of the Native Americans had been forced out and moved to other states.

The first known **settlement** by non-Native Americans was in 1631, by William Claiborne. In 1691, Maryland became a royal colony under England. In 1776, Maryland along with the rest of the Union declared its independence from England.

The **American Revolution** took place between the United States and England. Maryland played an important part in the war. The United States won the war and gained independence. On April 28, 1788, Maryland became the seventh state of the United States.

In 1791, Maryland gave 60 miles of land to the United States government for the nation's capital. It became Washington D.C.

An early painting of a Native American village in Maryland.

B.C. to 1632

Early Land and People

 During the Ice Age, many thousands of years ago, Maryland was covered by huge glaciers. Many years later the ice began to melt and the land of Maryland formed. It formed thick forests, rivers, lakes, mountains, and valleys.

 The first known people to occupy Maryland were **Native Americans.**

 1608: The first non-Native American to explore what is now Maryland was Captain John Smith.

 1632: England controls the area. George Calvert, first Lord of Baltimore, dies. His son Cecilius takes over.

Maryland

B.C. to 1632

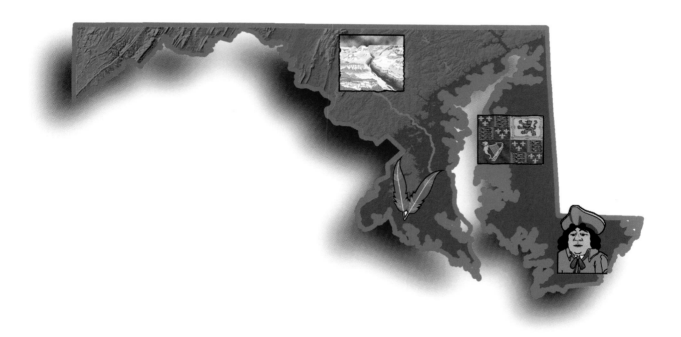

1776 to 1845

Statehood and Beyond

 1776: The Union, along with Maryland, declares its independence from England.

 1788: Maryland becomes the seventh state to join the Union.

 1791: Maryland gives part of its land to the United States so they can form Washington D.C.

 1814: Francis Scott Key writes United States national anthem, "The Star Spangled Banner," while being held as a prisoner on a British ship in Chesapeake Bay.

 1845: United States Naval Academy opens at Annapolis.

Maryland

1776 to 1845

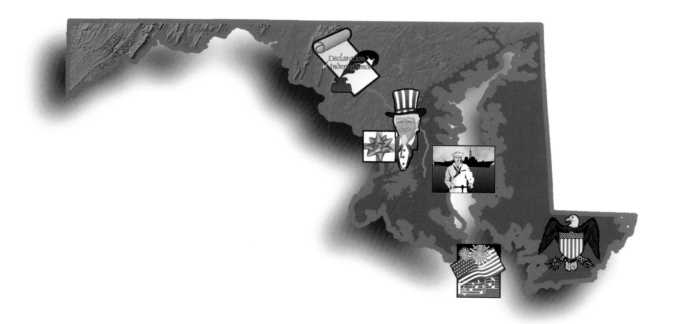

Russell Public Library
1 2 Main St.
P.O. Box 438
Russell, MA 01071
(413) 862-6221

1904 to Present

The 1900s

1904: The Great Baltimore Fire destroys much of the city.

1950: Friendship International Airport opened. It is now known as Baltimore-Washington International Airport.

1971: The Baltimore Colts win the Super Bowl.

1983: The Baltimore Orioles win their third World Series.

1995: Cal Ripken, Jr., of the Baltimore Orioles, makes baseball history by playing in 2,131 straight games.

Maryland

1904 to Present

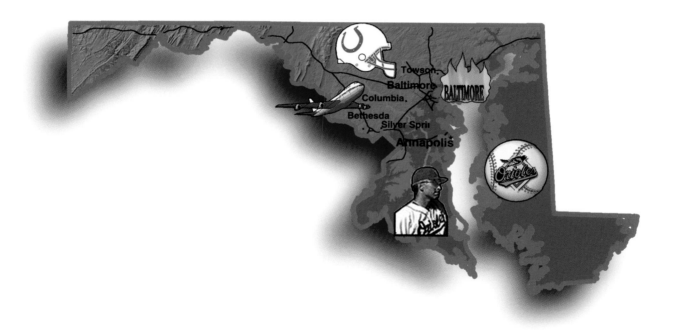

Maryland's People

There are about 4.8 million people living in the state of Maryland. The first known people to live in the state were **Native Americans**. Today, most people in the state are white. African Americans account for about 25 percent of the **population**.

Many well known people have made Maryland home. Johns Hopkins was born in Anne Arundel County in 1795. He started a grocery store and invested his money in the railroad. When he died in 1873, he left seven million dollars to the state to establish Johns Hopkins University and Hospital. The two places are famous throughout the world.

Francis Scott Key was born in Carrol County, Maryland. He wrote a poem called "In Defense of Fort M'Henry." He wrote it while watching the bombing of Fort McHenry in 1814, as a prisoner on a British ship in Chesapeake Bay.

The poem's name was changed to the "Star Spangled Banner." It was made into a song and became the United States national anthem in 1931.

Roger Brooke Taney was the attorney general of Maryland. He later served as Chief Justice of the Supreme Court from 1836 to 1864. He was part of the Dred Scott Decision, which said that slaves were not citizens.

Spiro Agnew was the **governor** of Maryland and later the Vice President of the United States under Richard Nixon. Agnew later resigned. Sargent Shriver, who was born in Westminster, was the losing Vice Presidential candidate in 1972. He is better known as John F. Kennedy's brother-in-law and his successful campaign manager.

Johns Hopkins

Spiro Agnew

Francis Scott Key

Splendid Cities

Maryland has many splendid cities in its state. Only one city in the state has more than 100,000 people. Most cities in Maryland are small, but still have many things to do and see.

The largest city, with over 700,000 people, is Baltimore. It has a major port on Chesapeake Bay. It is known as a historic city with monuments and museums.

A few colleges are in Baltimore with the most famous being Johns Hopkins University. The city is also home to Major League Baseball's Baltimore Orioles. The Orioles have had some excellent teams, winning the World Series in 1966, 1970, and 1983.

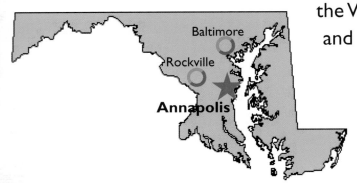

The next largest city, Rockville, has only 45,000 people. It is a residential city. Annapolis is the capital. It is on the Severn River. It is known for its United States Naval Academy. Like Baltimore, Rockville is known as a very historic city.

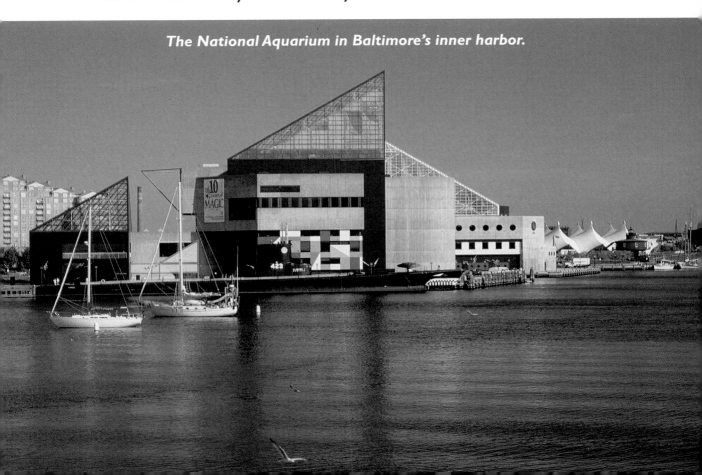

The National Aquarium in Baltimore's inner harbor.

Maryland's Land

Maryland has some of the most beautiful and diverse land in the country. The state sits on the **Atlantic Ocean**. Inland there are rivers, mountains, forests, and rich farmland. The state is divided into five different regions.

The largest region is the Coastal Plain, which covers the eastern half of the state. Streams cut through the low and flat countryside. At the center is Chesapeake Bay, which splits the region in half.

The Piedmont Plateau region is the second largest and is located just west of the Coastal Plain. The region is mainly rolling hills, and includes the areas of Baltimore and Washington D.C.

The Blue Ridge region is a small area that runs north to south in the central part of the state. Mountains and valleys cover the land. It has the Catoctin Mountain and the South Mountain.

The Valley and Ridge region is in a narrow neck in western Maryland. Its best feature is the outstanding Cumberland Valley, which is a part of the Great Appalachian Valley.

The Appalachian Plateau region covers the far western part of the state. It is a thickly forested valley and mountain area. The Backbone Mountain's jagged peaks can be seen in this area.

The Blackwater Refuge on Maryland's Eastern Shore.

Maryland at Play

Maryland is a great place to play. There are so many different things to do and see in this great state.

Ocean City is a famous **Atlantic Ocean resort**. There, a person can swim, surf, boat, and fish. The famous Preakness horse race is run in Baltimore.

Millions of **tourists** each year are attracted to Maryland's historic sites. Most people visit Baltimore, Annapolis, and Frederick. Each city has historic landmarks from United States history, especially those of the **American Revolution** and the Civil War.

Even presidents of the United States come to play in Maryland. Camp David, in scenic Catoctin Mountain Park in northern Maryland, is a place where many presidents have gone on vacation. The 200-acre, secret retreat is a beautiful resort for the president, his family, and invited guests.

Ocean City, Maryland, is a very popular vacation spot.

Maryland at Work

The people of Maryland must work to make money. There are many kinds of jobs that people do in the state. Because of the millions of visitors each year to Maryland, a lot of the people work in service jobs. Service means to work in hotels, **resorts**, restaurants, and stores.

About 10 percent of the people in the state work in the **manufacturing industry**. A lot of workers make electronic parts, like the parts that are in your television or stereo.

Some people are farmers. People raise cows for their milk and meat. Farmers in Maryland also grow corn and soybeans. Many people in Maryland fish. In Chesapeake Bay, fishermen catch clams, crabs, and oysters.

People in Maryland also cut trees so the wood can be made into lumber. Others work as **miners** under ground. Some of the most valuable **minerals** found in Maryland are stone, sand, gravel, clay, and coal.

There are wonderful things to do and see in the great state of Maryland. Because of its natural beauty, people, and land, Maryland is a great place to visit, live, work, and play.

Fishermen catching oysters on the Choptank River.

Fun Facts

• The highest point in the state is Backbone Mountain. It is 3,360 feet (1,024 meters). The lowest point is near Oakland. It is only about 350 feet (107 m).

• Maryland is a very small state. Only eight other states are smaller than Maryland in land size. Its land covers only 9,838 square miles (25,480 sq km). About 4.8 million people live there, which is a lot of people for such a small space.

• In 1830, Maryland completed the first railroad in the United States to carry passengers and freight. It was 13 miles (21 kilometers) long. It ran between Baltimore and Ellicott's Mills.

• In 1844, the first telegraph line in the United States was installed in Baltimore. It linked the city of Baltimore with the nation's capital, Washington D.C.

Samuel Morse, inventor of the telegraph.

Glossary

American Revolution: a war that gave the United States its independence from Great Britain.

Atlantic Ocean: one of a few large seas that surround continents. This one borders the entire east coast of the U.S. including Maryland.

Border: the line between neighboring states, countries, or waters.

Fertile: dirt that is fertile can grow plants very well.

Governor: the highest elected official in the state.

Industry: many different types of businesses.

Manufacture: to make things by machine in a factory.

Minerals: things found in the earth, such as rock, diamonds, or coal.

Miners: people who work underground to get minerals.

Native Americans: the first people who were born in and occupied North America.

Population: the number of people living in a certain place.

Resort: a place to vacation that has fun things to do.

Settlement: a place where people start their own city and live.

Tourists: people who travel for pleasure.

Internet Sites

Historic St. Mary's City Maryland's First Capital 634-1695
http://www.webgraphic.com/HSMC/index.htm
Historic St. Mary's City is an exciting mix of colorful living history and fascinating archaeology, all set in a beautiful tidewater landscape. With miles of walking trails and scenic river views, historic St. Mary's City is indeed a special place where "Time & Tide Meet."

MARYLAND LOYALISTS and the American Revolution
http://www.erols.com/candidus/index.htm
The saga of Marylanders loyalty to England is definitely one of the untold stories of the American Revolution. Loyalists in general are greatly misunderstood by the citizens of the 20th century.

These sites are subject to change. Go to your favorite search engine and type in Maryland for more information.

PASS IT ON
Tell Others Something Special About Your State
To educate readers around the country, pass on interesting tips, places to see, history, and little unknown facts about the state you live in. We want to hear from you!
To get posted on ABDO & Daughters website E-mail us at "mystate@abdopub.com"

Index

RUSSELL PUBLIC LIBRARY